PURGE

A TRUE STORY

DENISE YOUNG

authorHOUSE®

AuthorHouse™
1663 Liberty Drive
Bloomington, IN 47403
www.authorhouse.com
Phone: 1 (800) 839-8640

Published by AuthorHouse 11/30/2016

ISBN: 978-1-5246-5283-8 (sc)
ISBN: 978-1-5246-5284-5 (e)

Library of Congress Control Number: 2016918000

Print information available on the last page.

Any people depicted in stock imagery provided by Thinkstock are models,
and such images are being used for illustrative purposes only.
Certain stock imagery © Thinkstock.

This book is printed on acid-free paper.

Dedication

I'd like to dedicate this book to those who have gone through or is going through disrespect, abused or mistreatment of any kind. I pray that God give you freedom and peace.

Acknowledgement

I thank God for this opportunity and the gift to write my story. To my sons David and Paul, thank you! Thank you for all of your love and support during my writing process. To Paul, I want to thank you for listening as I needed your opinion, encouragement, challenging me not give up and a shoulder to cry on. To David, I want to thank you for listening, your support, your opinions, Godly advice, and challenging me to do my best. Also, for being a shoulder to cry on. I love my "Pillars" so much! I thank God for you both. To my brothers Donald and Jonathan, thank you for encouraging me to write. To my co-workers Jim, Tracy, and Scott, who took time out to read my work and give your opinions and support. Thank you! To Khaisha, thank you for your support and encouragement; your questions, which challenged me more and for giving me a new nickname I will always cherish, "Ms. Poetic". Thank you!

"Exclusive"

Dear Lord, I was yours exclusive for years. Attacks, literally, kept me in fear and tears. I loved you since I was a little girl. But the devil on the other hand was always sending for my "pearls". Somehow you gave me strength to resist him in every way. Yet he always returned to make me pay. Still small in stature, I eventually put the whole armor on. Shield in place; my feet ready to run this race. I ran faithful for years. Then it became time to grow. Without thinking, I laid my shield down though! Wasn't aware of the new snare there waiting for me. The trap prepared to cut off my destiny. I decided to rest my feet. I didn't think anything of it! My helmet pushed over my eyes. I didn't see what was above it! In my mind was placed years of bad memories in cascades! A war began that lasted for decades! I wasn't completely protected and no match for the blades. I looked at the deep cuts, gashes and bruises on my feet. Making me feel at times, I was in defeat. I asked you for forgiveness along the way. So, in your hands of protection I'd stay. Father, your love, grace and mercy has covered me. At this stage in my walk with you, I know it's your will that I stay free. Free to choose wrong or right. Free to let go and give you total reigns of my life's fight. Free to become the woman I'm evolving to be. Free, with a lot of love, happiness, joy and peace. Free to have a personal relationship with you. Now being "Exclusive" to you, in this life, I'll make it victoriously through. Amen.

"The Feather"

As I sit here thinking of you; heart full of warm thoughts. I look at the floor and then I saw... "The feather", all dressed in white; peacefully lying on its side; unchanged by the feet that passed it by. The feather that came from you, has attached itself to my shoe. Oh how I miss you to, looking at "The feather" that remind me of you.

"My Night Owl"

I'm sitting quietly, looking up at the stars. I'm thinking, how beautiful! Smiling so big; my heart at peace and I'm feeling very special. I look over at "My Night Owl", who has created all these great emotions inside of me. I'm looking at his face, so handsome, calm and at peace. I feel secure as we relax in the pleasant night air. I look up and see a constellation shaped like a diamond with two tails and a star on each of them. I slept off and on throughout the night, as I gaze at the moon and the stars for light. It was the best rest we've had sitting up in a while. I'm looking forward to more nights like this, with "My Night Owl."

"A New Day"

As I lay me down to go to sleep, my eyes filled with tears, I continue to weep. I'm thinking back over my life up to now. I realized I must rise somehow. The pain inside, for years did not go away. As I prayed to God, He let me know, "daughter, it's "A New Day". So, as I listened to the lyrics of "Love", a song introduced to me by a friend. I hear in my spirit God saying, "You win. See with me all things are possible to him that believe. Let go of your past and give your life back to me." It's a new day. I am free. I'm stepping forward into my God given destiny.

(QUOTE): "Real Peace"

"There is nothing like the peace you receive when into
God's hands you hold and to His word you cling."

(QUOTE): "Fairy Tale"

"Even when he's not trying, he turns into her Prince.
Although to him, fairytales makes no sense".

"Bounce Back"

The worst thing you can do is strip a woman of her gain. Removing her assets, causing her pain. Taking away her pride and joy, like you punish a child by taking away their special toy. It's like giving her a gut punch! She feels the pain and anguish! That pain is real! Hurting her so deep inside, breaking her bit by bit and all of her pride. She smiles to keep from crying. She laughs to keep her inside, from dying. She talks about it in around about ways; leaving her listener in a daze and asking, "What is she really talking about? How long has she been going through it?" She leaves her mark on the heart and minds of those who will listen to it. The worst thing you can do is strip a woman of her gain. Now she has nothing but her pain...

(QUOTE): "Be Good to Her"

"Be good to her. For her "karma" will show you it was worth it.
She learns how to bounce back and never have to explain"

"Joy"

"Joy"-**J**ust a smile **on** your face. **Y**ou go through life full of grace.

"Joy"- Not **J**udging anyone. **O**ne love for all. **Y**es you love everyone without hesitation or stall.

"Joy"- **J**uggling life like everyone else. **O**wning your responsibilities, **Y**et trusting the one who gives joy freely. **J**oy **O**n **Y**our life is a good feeling.

(QUOTE): "JOY"

"JUST OWN YOU!"

"PRAISE"

Praise is what I love to do; to set me free; to get me through; the trials in life that beat on me; those that weigh me down, and cause my face to wear a frown. Praise is the key that unlocks the doors to the blessings I've been waiting for. Praise gives the peace of mind I need to carry on; the joy my heart receives when I'm all alone. Praise is what I love to do; it sets me free to receive the blessings God has for me.

(QUOTE): "PRAISE HIM"

"Look up and praise Him until you praise through. He
will send His blessings down upon you."

"I'm A Writer To"

I'm a writer to. I always have been. See life kept getting in the way of me and the thoughts within. Did I mention I'm an illustrator to? I've been drawing since I was a kid. I'm good at it to! It's another gift that was just hid. I enjoy writing about real life with a rhyme. That makes it last over time. I pour my heart out! Yeah! "Spill the beans". You know the saying? You know what I mean. I'm a writer to. In case you didn't know, putting my life on paper but, with a rhyming flow.

(QUOTE): "Share Your Gift"

Share your gift and talents with others. It may be your gift or talent
that unlocks the gift or talent in your sister or brother.

"While You Were Away"

While you were away, I missed you. While you were away, I kissed you with my heart. While you were away, I cried for you. While you were away, I prayed for you to. While you were away, I dreamed about you. While you were away, I tried to talk to you. While you were away, you ignored me totally. While you were away, you pushed me away with your attitude solely. While you were away, you smiled and laughed with someone else. While you were away, you left me to pray all by myself. While you were away, you stayed awake off and on throughout the night. While you were away, you talked away until daylight. While you were away, I tried to connect with you. While you were away, I held on to you for dear life. While you were away, Instead, I had to give up the fight. While you were away, I came to realize this; While you were away, it wasn't me that you missed.

"Hold a Place in Your Heart for Me"

"Hold a place in your heart for me", he said. With pain in his voice as in regret. Replying positively, I knew things had changed. You see, I had to pray that love away. The kind that only your soul and spirit obey. Sometimes we meet that person who we know is "the one". That perfect fit. He was it. We lost that love through years and life. Decisions we made in misery and strife. Of course, we have to put the blame where it belongs. But of late that "old love" won't leave him alone.

"Don't Pretend If You Don't"

Don't pretend if you don't love me. But yet have the need to be loved by me. Don't pretend if you don't care for me; being selfish, like, "this is the place to be!" Don't pretend if you don't like me. Knowing you can't stand it when I come around. On your face you put such a frown. It's sad to say but I loved you anyway. Giving you a lot of what you didn't deserve and to get the reaction from you of perturbed. Knowing that when I walked into your life, I had already been through misery and strife. I tried to tell you what I had been through. But you didn't want to hear it because you knew what you had planned to do. Then you said you didn't know anything about me. Well, that's your fault. You walked into my life just to take from me. Now this is how "karma" will unfold, by giving back to me what you stole. I'm here now and you're there. I saw the "good man" in you. We could've been the perfect pair. But you pretended to be real when you knew you weren't. Sending both our lives up a whole new current. See the time two people share getting to know one another in the beginning; you can't get that time back! Time that's just wasted from your lives; still ending in lack. Well, I've learned from this if you won't. "Don't pretend if you don't!"

"Tears"

How many tears would it take to fill a lake; of a life, life did take? How many tears would it take to fill a sea? Giving back the joy and happiness life took like a thief? How many tears would it take to flood the world? To gain compensation of One's life in hope, love and pearls? How many tears of joy can One shed for the return of happy thoughts in their head? How many tears? You may ask; do I have to cry before I transition from this life? Well, there's GOOD NEWS from heaven! I want you to know; God have seen every tear and He has not given you the spirit of fear. Trust in Him with all your might and know everyone of your battles He will fight.

(QUOTE): "Misery"

"Misery doesn't always want company. It just needs
a body bigger than itself to spill into."

"He Looked at Me" (part I)

He looked at me with discuss in his eyes. As if I'm the reason he despise. Always saying, "black women have an attitude." No. Just discarded by black men like you. See I love my black Kings with a passion. But I've been so hurt, used and abused by them in such a fashion. But I've realized that some of them were just like me. Hurting, used and abused by someone else you see. So, as he looked at me with despise in his eyes; it hurt! I can't lie! But I just kept it moving as he passed by with that discussed look in his eyes.

"He Looked At Me" Part II

He looked at me with a new look in his eyes. He smiled, tooted the horn and waved his hand this time. A new look I tell you! It was refreshing to see him be so kind and it blew mind! To the point it made me want to boast; how I knew it was just a matter of time that the look of discuss would one day be a ghost! It felt good to know he had changed. (We had yet to speak, let alone me be the blame!) You see as I said before. I love my black Kings with a passion! Now, he passes by me on this fashion: "Hey! How you doing?" Me, "Good? Thank you! And You?" "Not too bad! Glad to know you're doing well to!"

"Don't Complain"

Don't complain about the people who judge you; because you know all they say, is what you do. Stop trying to fight those who can live life straight. The plan God has for you, you chose to abate. Just living so "footloose and fancy free!" Not living up to what He called you to be. So don't complain about what people say about you. Because you're the one who chose to do what you do.

"REALITY (He or She)"

Is (he/she) truly going in the same direction as you? Or in the end, you'll find that you still are two? Is (his/her) passion lining up with yours? Or in the end you'll find (he/she) is just a chore? Is the conversation you two hold got you grinning? Or in the end you'll realized you're not winning? Does the connection you're feeling seem life lasting? Does it seem "too good to be true" and got you basking? Is (he/she) challenging you to greatness? Or will you find that "it's every man for themselves", in their heart, is what they say? Do (he/she) complement you just by a look? Or in every way with nothing forsook? Do (he/she) love you when you have nothing to give? Hoping in (his/her) heart "one day, happy ever after you'll live." Is your promise to (him/her) an unfazed position? Or will (he/she) in the end leave you wishing? Do (he/she) promote the best in you? Or in the end you're left feeling blue? Don't waste your time with someone connected to two; for in "UNITY", there's ONE. That's what will help you make it through. So, I've decided to stay with God all the way; waiting patiently; He'll send my King some day. Now what do you say?

"knock It OFF!"

Have you ever been with your significant other and felt there was distance? Not knowing why there were but, behind the scenes was a lot of resistance. You love them; them loving someone else. Not telling you the truth of their heart thus continuing the curse. Ah! They're wasting both of your time to! Trying to keep their "knock off" plan and that "knock off plan" is YOU! They won't admit it. Neither will they let you tell them that this is true! Weather they admit it or not, it's killing you! There's many ways of making a person feel like they're dying inside. Just living life we fine this out! But being put to death in such a silent way is very cunning, no doubt! "knock it off!" You'll tell them. "You don't have the right!" Giving them another chance, only to continue the fight. Come on people! Knock it off! Live the truth! Be blunt! If you're not with the one you want, don't put up a fake front! That's not fair to someone thinking what they've found is true. It's hard enough finding someone to spend quality time with; let alone be used by YOU! It's so sad people's hearts are this cold. Not taking the time to heal so they can be rid of the old: old ways, old thoughts, old charms, and old faults! This is why TRUST is hard to maintain. So many are guilty and don't want to admit and carry their blame.

"This Part of ME"

This part of me you see is the me, I need to be. For this is the part of me that somehow got suppressed as I matured. Life is funny that way. Whether through life itself or the people we interact with everyday. Both can rob you of the most important facts of you in some way. The Fact: that you are worthy of respect no matter your age. You don't have to accept people's evil ways, and then just turn the page! Moving from chapter to chapter without relief kills a part of you, your truth and belief. The Fact: that you are beautiful or handsome; hands down! But if not life, it's people causing your pleasant face to wear a frown. One otherwise wouldn't even appear but, the pain get so great it causes you to shed many tears. The Fact: that you have a divine destiny but, you become so broken, shattered even, that you can't see what use to be. The Fact: that life can be beautiful but, it becomes a handful. The tears become less; the heart is now sick because hope has been deferred too long; Love may still linger but, when love is never reciprocated, life is drained, numbing the heart that use to produce love on its own. This part of me you see is real. (LOL!!!) Some may think "I thought I knew her?" But, there's a part of all of us that needs to evolve at some point. If not, it keeps us from our divine destiny. So, with that being said, the me you see should be read: You are beautiful! With a divine destiny! Your life will be beautiful with many years of love, laughter and life you see! So here you have it. Just another part of ME. In a quest to be FREE.

"He Called Me Two-Faced"

He called me Two-Faced. Having a smile like mine isn't rare. It only shows the pain and burdens I've had to bare. My left side shows the pain; my right side joy proclaimed. I look at my photos and I see it myself. I don't need to be reminded by no one else. It's not the laugh in your face, talk behind your back two-face. It's the I have a story to tell of my own self. The living, breathing, caring, burden baring face that is seen yet with such wealth. Wealth in knowledge, wisdom and love. Receiving mercy and grace from above. A face like this can't make it any other way. For the woes of life have certainly been put on display. But, there are triumphs, victories to! With that being said, there are lots of good days I have to look forward to. My victories you'll see! To God be the glory on my behalf. For He loves ME!

"My Faithfulness"

My faithfulness is full. On the brink of disaster. All I wanted
to do is give him some joy and laughter.

"A Strong Person You Say?"

A strong person you say? Strong should have been my first name. I've been through such a war, "Weak"? I can't even claim. A strong person you say? I've been hated, with no fault of my own but I've loved hard anyway. Been despised for petty, simple minded causes! Yet I've lent a helping hand. Giving and sharing like a "Boss" of Bosses. A strong person you say? Strong should have been my middle name! Yes I said it! When God lent you ME, He was showing you what strong could be. Not just because of what I've been through but, how He has prepared ME to be strong to befriend and love YOU! And I Pause...

"Now That We're Here"

Our life's journey leads us in many places, directions and situations. Where we end up is our choice. Now that we are here, the choice is yours to resolve. I've exhausted all of mine. I'm giving you the choice to be kind. I just ask that you give me what we both know is mine. I was all in and you were always out. That's what this is all about. Now that we're here, let's resolve this relationship once and for all. Without a meeting of the minds, we were headed for this fall. Well now that all minds are clear. We can begin by saying, "Now that we're here"; I can finally admit that my love for you just wasn't your perfect fit. Letting go is for the best. But you have to admit I stood the tests. Though many they were, I passed them all. Too bad we had to take this type of fall.

"Let Go"

There comes a time when you have to let go. Knowing how sometimes life flow. You have to learn how to live and let live. If it's meant for you it'll give. Give in like return back to you; for it's in this love, selfishness can't shine through. So be at peace within yourself. Let go! It's the greatest feeling and good for your health.

(QUOTE): "Freeing You To Receive"

"Sometimes you free you to receive your breakthrough."

"Let Go and Embrace"

Hey: Don't waste life on trivial things. Life is too precious to miss all of its blessings. Leave the past behind. "Some clocks we should not rewind." Love on you today. Let real love find its way. If you're willing to let go of the old and embrace the possibilities of the new, who could say your dreams couldn't come true? So, let go and embrace what's been waiting for you. For who knows what all those possibilities could do...

"These Two Sticks"

These two sticks fell from a tree. They both hit the ground at the same time you see. The sun was shining but, it began to rain. One clung onto the other. Both were in pain. The one was in pain from the scare of the fall and the other from the impact of it all. Then the rain stopped, allowing the frightened stick to loosen the grip. Looking down at the other saying, "boy what a trip!" Sharing their life while in the tree, they had no clue how sweet life could be. Falling together and surviving it all. They realized true love and partnership. "Boy what a fall!"

(QUOTE): "Falling Together"

"When you fall together, you RISE stronger!

(QUOTE): "Tough Gain"

"This pain will be rewarded greatly."

"Girl"

Girl when are you going to learn? For his love you yearn! Girl, swallow your pride! For inside of you is where your treasure abides. Girl open your eyes and see. In you, there's a lot of possibility! Girl, it's ok to just walk, sometimes, the other way! Never stay where you're not wanted! It's yours not his heart that feels taunted. Always speak your mind! Girl don't give anybody the opportunity to put you at the end of the line. You're too good for all that! Being in that person's life now, isn't where it's at. Opportunity for better is where true love and life breeds. It's in that one that has all your needs! Girl you can start over; give it some time. Staying with him won't make your life worth a dime. You can have all the riches in the world. If you're not happy, you'll feel like the one who's lost their real diamonds and pearls. Don't fake how you feel for no one. If they care at all for you, you won't have to. Girl, make your life count for more than" a dime a dozen!" Stand out, shine bright and be the one that make him fight! Fight for you! Your attention, your smile, your dimensions, your likes, your laugh, your love, your dreams and goals. Your passion, your fashion, your eating habits to! They say a way to a man's heart is through his stomach. At least for some that's true. Your life is yours, live it to the fullest. For when you've earned from what you've learned, those things NOMORE will you yearn.

"Dear Heart"

Dear Heart: you're so strong! I don't know how you go on. They say you're mainly made of muscle. That I can believe. I don't know how you keep beating as much as you've had to bleed. I guess when God made you; He put some extra fibers in there. Because, there's no way you could go on beating like you do with the burdens you've had to bare. There has to be a bright side to your surviving. Somehow you just keep on thriving. Yes! I'm so glad you're mine. You are one of a kind. They don't come equipped like you much anymore. I'm encouraged at that thought; knowing there's more life to explore. Heart's reply: Oh yeah! God put extra "Purkinjes" in there to make sure those heavy burdens you could bare. Smile wide my friend. Let the sun shine bright from within. When you go through your day or your night, it is God that will help you win the fight.

(QUOTE): "Be True To You"

Besides God You know YOU!

"This Time"

There's no love loss in a love that was never found. Infinity couldn't even trace its steps. It was so hidden in the locks of "This Time", that its very weight was untraceable. Then because of its absence, there wasn't even a shadow. Meaning there was no sunshine. But "this time" there was only HOPE. Hope is a very good thing but when time put its shade on it, it tends to fade bit by bit, until it forgets it ever exist. But "This Time" COURAGE...well courage died along with PRIDE when the last deluge of disaster hit. HA! Oh yeah! TENACITY!? Wow! Now Tenacity could've held all the rest together but "This Time"...boy did it put a hurting on those strings! I mean! "This Time" tugged and pulled so fiercely at the threads of Tenacity, it became unrecognizable. Then bit by bit all the rest began to fade away with "This Time". But then there is WISDOM! Hahaha! Thank God for wisdom! See with time, wisdom only gets better! It was through the loss of love where there was no love to loose, wisdom begun to germinate. Now "This Time" love is found. It's alive and growing strong. Patiently awaiting the reciprocation of a deserved love that will never fade; stand strong; using knowledge that only knowledge knows how to give; stemming from the wisdom that "This Time" did let live. See it's through Love all (Hope, Joy, Peace, Pride, Tenacity and Courage) are regained and, through Wisdom, Knowledge and Understanding they can remain.

"Take a Chance"

Don't give up on YOU! You are important to. Hold onto that hope! The one that's saying, "Nope!" I'm worth it; I deserve it; God put this love in me! I'm free for someone to love ME. Nope! To all the negative thoughts that come day by day; to those looking, watching just to say, "He or she" is too old now his or her time has passed. That's cold! Senseless statements made, if you need to ask! Give your life a chance, to take a chance on the good things life has to offer. Vacation: take as many as you can! Adventures: the sky is the limit! Road trips: drive until your little heart's content! Fly until your money is spent; float! Sail! Swim! Take a chance on people. Don't judge everyone by the few bad ones you've came across. That's part of life, your lesson and their loss.

"Today"

Today I feel more alone than ever. Though that could be a good change in a heart and mind so cleaver. I have yet many things I'd like to do; and love is still on that list to. Today has been kind of weird; though my heart and mind hasn't veered; those things I know I'm suppose to take care of and attending to the things I'm given to do from above. Today can only get better; it had a gloomy start due to life's chatter. I guess God's silence is saying, "I've opened the door walk out! It's okay if you shout. I love your praise anyway! So go ahead and let today be a great day!

"Life Is Funny Like That"

Life is funny like that. How things come full circle. Sometimes it takes longer than expected and one day you are just surprised. I had the pleasure of speaking to an old friend the other day. We caught up on quite a lot of the years lost between the last times we spoke. Literally! Speaking was all I would allow to happen between us. I found out after all these years my gut instincts was correct. I'm not surprised! It usually is. We laughed, shared history of our lives, weather, our plans, desires, hopes and dreams. Conclusion: We're still two good people, living different lives, desires, hopes, goals and dreams.

"S.M.H."

S.M.H. we use this a lot. When happy or sad; Frustrated or glad; Even when we cough! S.M.H. just comes in handy. I like to use it myself. It expresses something deeper than words can say. It's often used, instead of on the nose of one, your hand(s) you'd prefer to lay. S.M.H. is often enough expression to give. It simply helps you live and let live. S.M.H. is simply meaning shake my head. We tend to do it a lot. Sometimes it's the best comeback you've got.

"Brighter Side"

Life could be worse. So, I'll say thank you first, for all the things you've brought me through. Giving me insight on what I must do. Letting hope continue to inspire, the love in me not to retire. The joy that I can't explain, though my heart is yet in pain. Sometimes I laugh uncontrollable. My life is in your hands. You hold me. Thank you for the brighter side of things. I'm looking forward to this New Year and all the joy it brings with laughter and cheer.

"I Imagine Joy"

The joy of joys, I imagine it to be. Happiness, laughter and peace inside of me. No complaints. Lots of cheer, giggles and giddiness throughout the year. Now no one knows how long this joy will last. But with every moment the joy will pass. In life there are ups and downs. Know that joy though is somewhere around. "You choose happiness", people may say. Bring joy back in many ways. Spending time alone doing what you love to do. Or sharing precious moments with family and friends to. Caring for the sick and shut in. Feeding those who are hungry; housing the homeless or just pondering life for a solution to its sundry. Joy is a wonderful thing! To have joy, it's the life that life is supposed to bring.

(QUOTE)"Joy Comes"

"Joy comes in many ways. Choose any one or all of them".

"Peace"

Peace, be still. It's time to do His divine will. You are not your own. So, this battle, leave it alone. He is here for you. Grace and mercy given, that's true. But one thing you need to know, how much He love you so! He died; He gave His life. He made the ultimate sacrifice. So you can have a right to the "tree of life". Peace, be still and know that He is God! Let the preparation of your feet be shod; being more ready to hear than to sacrifice. The battle is the Lords'! Let Him fight! Peace, be still with all your might. You are why He made the ultimate sacrifice.

"Speak Life"

That's right brother! Speak life into your family! That's what you do! Bring hope back to your family, that which the evil one has tried to tear into. Speak life into your spouse. Tell her how much you're willing to do. Pray to God that He'll restore your love. That only He at this point can send from above. Tell her how beautiful she is; how well she does the things she does. Tell her how you want to become one again and not two. Tell your seed how much they're loved. How smart they are and how the symbol of peace is a dove. Let them see you love on their mother. Showing them how much they should love one another. Family in the end is all you got. Speak life into them. If you want family to thrive you must give it a shot. Speak LIFE.

(QUOTE)"New Eyes"

"At some point you must see life through New Eyes."

"Purpose"

Purpose is said to be "the reason something is done or created or for which something exist." "Have as one's intention or objective. Something done with purpose has determination behind it." When what you do have a purpose, there is an aim or intentional plan in mind. What's the purpose for why people really hurt some people and choose to give others the utmost respect? Why would one hate another for just existing in their presence and welcome others with open arms? Love is a choice to. One of the best emotions one can experience! Yet because of the lack of understanding it fully or at all, the purpose for which it has between two individuals can be grossly dismissed. When purpose is given to an individual from God, He places all that is needed in them to began the journey and complete it as well.

(QUOTE)"Just Roarrr..."

"Don't be the snake! Be the Lion! Roar and get on with it!"
(By: Paul L. Robinson 6-2015)

(QUOTE)"Chumps"

"Living the life of a true Christian aint for Chumps"
(By: David A. Young 8-7-2016)

"The Switch"

Looking over my life like there's no tomorrow. Casting off those cares; the ones we borrow. Taking inventory of the good and the bad. Reminiscing of the pleasures that I've had. Grabbing hold to my "purpose" like it's my last breath; realizing parts of my life could've put me to death. Having joy, faith and peace right now; is giving me the strength to break free somehow. My conscience cleans, having no fear. It's feeling mighty good to be sitting here! Thinking of my destiny, the one that was meant be. I'm beginning to live out the life that was meant for me.

"Wow"

Wow! That could have been me! Sleeping on the streets with no shoes on my feet or food to eat. Wow! I've got to look back. Thinking how my life got off track. The drugs, the drinks! People saying, "You better not blink!" That last situation was a bad bought. Wondering to myself, man, how did I get out? Peace? I couldn't find none, until I sought the one who took me off the run and even after that I began to slowly drift off track. (SMH) What an amazing life! Filled with such pain, misery and strife. One day I made a choice. I took heed to the one who gave me a voice. Wow! Now I'm free. The bad realized. All of it could have been ME!

Purge: A True Story

Biography

Hello my name is Denise Young. I'm the only girl born to the union of two wonderful parents. Mr. and Mrs. Donald Ray and Ann Stowers Young. Two great brothers. Mr. Donald Young and Mr. Jonathan Young. I am a proud mother of two wonderful, handsome young men. I call them my "Pillars". Mr. David Young and Mr. Paul Robinson. Whom I love so much. I am Aunt and Great-Aunt to a beautiful group of Nieces. Also, a handsome group of Nephews and Great-Nephews. I began to write at a young age in grade school. Writing became a hobby after a while because, I loved to make words have a meaningful rhyme. I became involved in church, school and life's activities and, my poems and short stories began to fade away. I've recently began writing again after years of trials and errors of life. Much heart break in relationships. Many joys and triumphs, as well. I was inspired to publish my first book at this time of my transition. My youngest just graduated 2015. So, I decided to write my story in a unique form. My story in many quotes and poems. I'm enjoying this writing process and look forward to more book publishing projects in the near future.

Purge: A True Story

Introduction

"Purge: A True Story", is my real life story. I began to write poems and quotes again after having years of trials and tribulations. Painfully, they put me into a great transition of life while in my mid forties. After being a devoted wife and mother for years. I'm now a divorced, single woman, who has raised two grown sons. I decided to search for my position in my life's journey. Although I've experienced many heartbreaking issues, I also have plenty of happy days. These happy days allowed me to regroup. Putting my story on paper, in poetic form, helped me to reflect, rejuvenate and release it all to keep pressing forward. So, what unfolds in the pages of this book volume I, is the truth of me. But, sometimes this is how life can be. I'm giving God the glory for allowing me to survive these storms. My happy days have given me encouragement to share my stories, in the form of my quotes and my poems.

Printed in the United States
By Bookmasters